One Jordan

One Jordan

How to Connect With High Performing Individuals

Chris Welton

Published by Game Changer Publishing

Paperback ISBN: 978-1-963793-01-7
Hardcover ISBN: 978-1-963793-02-4
Digital: ISBN: 978-1-963793-03-1

GC GAME CHANGER
PUBLISHING
www.GameChangerPublishing.com

DEDICATION

This book is dedicated to my wife Nicki. She gave me the support and confidence to write this book. I love you Nicki.

NLEE

Read This First

Just to say thanks for buying and reading my book, I would like to give you a few free bonus gifts, no strings attached!

To Download Your Free Gifts, Scan the QR Code:

One Jordan

*How to Connect With High
Performing Individuals*

Chris Welton

GC GAME CHANGER
PUBLISHING

www.GameChangerPublishing.com

Foreword

Connection is the essence of humanity, and how we forge these connections can be as varied as the shoes we choose to wear. In a world teeming with voices, ideas, and relentless information streams, standing out from the crowd is both an art and a formidable challenge. Connection, real and profound, requires more than surface-level engagement; it calls for innovation, courage, and a willingness to venture beyond the familiar.

I've spent three decades exploring the depths of behavioral neuroscience, unraveling the secrets of change, sales, leadership, and influence. As the bestselling author of *Amplify Your Influence*, I've witnessed firsthand the extraordinary power that comes from understanding the human mind. Yet, even within this vast landscape of human potential, certain ideas resonate with a unique and compelling clarity.

One such idea emerged while visiting my good friend Brad Lea's office. Faced with how to connect with high-profile individuals, the concept was simple yet audacious: send one Jordan shoe with a note that read, *"If you want the second one, give me a call."* It was an ingenious idea that broke through convention, offering a fresh and intriguing approach to networking.

Chris Welton, the mastermind behind *One Jordan*, seized this idea with a relentless commitment and fervor that I find both inspiring and reflective of his character. As a distinguished performance coach, dynamic speaker, and expert connector, Chris embodies the qualities that make genuine leaders stand apart: creativity, determination, and the courage to act.

Fear of rejection, that universal barrier, often stifles our most innovative thoughts. However, in Chris's world, fear is confronted head-on, replaced with a courageous pursuit of excellence. His journey, so vividly chronicled in this remarkable book, transcends mere novelty; it's a testament to the power of thinking beyond the ordinary, stepping out of comfort zones, and embracing the unknown.

Chris's story resonates with me, not only because of its inventive approach but also for its alignment with the principles I've explored in my work. It's a tangible illustration of how understanding human behavior and leveraging it with creativity can yield transformative results. His fearless commitment to standing out, connecting authentically, and pushing forward is a beacon for anyone navigating the complex world of networking, leadership, and personal development.

As you journey through the pages of *One Jordan*, you'll experience more than a captivating narrative; you'll embark on a path of self-discovery and innovation. Chris becomes your guide, leading you into a world where individuality shines, persistence pays off, and your unique voice finds its place.

The challenge of standing out, the fear that often holds us back, the courage to overcome it, and the relentless pursuit of excellence are common themes in Chris's work and my explorations. Together, they form a tapestry that invites you to create your unique narrative one audacious step at a time.

Embrace the journey with *One Jordan*. Let the transformation begin, guided by the wisdom, courage, and relentless commitment of Chris Welton, a man who has not only walked the talk but has also danced it in a pair of unmatched shoes.

In pursuing extraordinary connections, remember that it all starts with you. Chris's story invites us all to think, act, and connect in a way that resonates with our authentic selves. Whether you're taking the first step in your career, seeking to elevate your influence, or looking to forge connections that matter, this book is a roadmap to the next level of your life.

As someone who has dedicated his life to understanding the dynamics of influence and change, I see in Chris's work a reflection of what's possible when creativity meets courage, when ideas meet execution, and when one shoe becomes the symbol of a movement.

– Rene Rodriguez, Bestselling author of *Amplify Your Influence*

Table of Contents

"Let's talk about the thoughts in my head and how I kept a growth mindset."

"After all, fortune favors the bold."

Introduction

I wrote this book for individuals trying to connect with someone they feel is out of their league. Someone doing what you want to do, but you're unsure how to contact them. I will share several stories throughout this book about how I connected with elite, high-performing individuals by simply sending a handwritten note and one shoe. Of course, the single Jordan shoe was always a brand new Jordan chosen specifically for that individual, which didn't hurt my cause. Even though it was one of the most iconic brands ever produced, you may still ask yourself, *Why did they respond to this guy?* The answer is simple—it was unique and bold. It sparked curiosity about who this guy thinks he is and his agenda. Wouldn't you wonder the same thing?

I'll be upfront and honest with you here. I'm the self-proclaimed king of R&D, which stands for "rip-off and duplicate." I heard the idea about the Jordan shoe from Brad Lea, who heard it from Rene Rodriguez. I took the idea and ran with it. The fact that Jordans, which you'll hear more about as you continue reading, and my love for the brand were involved felt like a sign to me—a sign that maybe I should pursue this incredible networking idea.

Let's break down the process and mindset that made this all come together and ultimately work. First, I created a list of people I wanted to connect with. Then, I looked at their social platforms to determine if they wore Jordans. Most had posted a photo or two of them wearing the iconic brand. Of course, you ask, "How did you get their shoe size?" There are several ways. For example, I sent a DM to an individual asking if they always preferred Jordan 1s because I had seen them wearing them in photos. He responded, "No, I prefer Jordan 3s." Before I got ahead of myself, it was a unique question, and I received a response. I mean, really, how many times have you DM'd someone and never received a response? I'm guessing a lot. So, my next question to this individual was, "Just curious, what size shoe do you wear?" He responded, and then I had his shoe size.

I've also reached out to the individual's assistant and, in one instance, acted like a customer on their website and put in the request. Once I had their shoe size, I purchased the Jordans I thought would best suit the individual and removed one shoe from the box. I wrote a handwritten letter requesting a 15-minute Zoom meeting in exchange for the other Jordan—a simple exchange of goods.

Let's talk about the thoughts in my head and how I kept a growth mindset. My first thought was, *What if they don't respond?* Followed by, *What do I do if they respond? Why would they even want to talk to Chris Welton? What if we get on Zoom, and I stare at them and don't know what to say? What if I go through all the steps and work to get the shoe size, pay for it, send the shoe, and then receive no response?* I realized that some would respond, and some wouldn't. So what? I'm going for it.

I remember the first shoe I sent. I was so excited and was confident I would get an instant response. I tracked the package, saw it was signed for, and expected my phone to ring. That didn't happen. I DM'd the individual multiple times, waiting for another response. I knew one of two things would happen. He would either appreciate my persistence, or I'd get blocked.

The next day, my phone rang. It was a number I didn't recognize, so I let it go to voicemail like most of us. After listening to it, I called him back immediately and set up what was to be the first of many Zoom calls. I'm still nervous each time I send out "One Jordan," and it still takes aggressive follow-up to get through sometimes. I'll wait with aggressive patience for a response.

In this book, I describe my many connections and the relationships built that will last a lifetime because of "One Jordan." If you want to level up your networking and connect with those high-level individuals you feel may be out of reach, take this blueprint and make it your own. *After all, fortune favors the bold.*

If you want to level up your networking and connect with those high-level individuals you dreamed about, take this blueprint and make it your own.

"When we walked into the Foot Locker, time stopped. The most beautiful shoes I had ever seen were right before me."

~

"I had my first pair of Jordans.
The love affair had begun."

CHAPTER ONE

Sneakers, Dreams and Grandma Margret

I remember the first time shoes meant something to me. It wasn't when I first walked as a toddler, but when I realized that what you put on your feet represented who you were. Up to that point, I would, of course, wear whatever shoes I was given. The brand or style didn't matter. What mattered was if they fit. I'm sure you remember going to the store to buy shoes as a kid and having the salesperson measure your foot on the cold metal device to determine what size shoe you needed from the rack. My little sister and I would get new shoes when school started. With any luck, they might last until summer. In the summer, I would go barefoot as much as possible or wear a pair of those dollar flip-flops from the "five-and-dime" because getting another pair of shoes soon was improbable.

When I started playing little league baseball, my mom took me to Kmart, and we would buy the least expensive pair of cleats we could find. You know the ones. They looked like Adidas but had five stripes instead of three, or they resembled Nike, but the swoosh was upside down. They were your basic knockoffs, made of plastic and vinyl, with no leather involved in their making. You get it.

Then, in fourth grade, it all changed. I went to my friend Mark's house for the first time, and he had a closet full of sneakers. I was amazed. He had more pairs of sneakers than I could count, and they all fit him. They were lined up along the wall, and all looked brand new. These were Nike, Adidas, and Converse shoes. I remember the smell of the leather; I didn't even know that was a thing. He was the first person I ever knew who had a shoe collection. I was in absolute awe. I ran home and couldn't wait to tell my mom.

Out of breath from running, I told her about Mark's shoes and that I wanted shoes like that. Her response was, "Mark is rich. You have to be rich to get shoes like that."

Well, even at my age, I knew we weren't rich. So, if I wanted shoes like Mark's, I would have to figure out how to make money myself, and that's precisely what I did.

When fifth grade started, I begged my mom to buy me name-brand shoes. My first pair of non-Kmart shoes was a pair of black high-top Converse Chuck Taylors. My mom took me to pick them out at Peoples Department Store. I remember feeling special wearing them on the first day of school. I even slept in them the night before.

My love affair with shoes had officially begun. From then on, I asked for shoes every birthday, Christmas, and whenever I expected a present. They were all I ever wanted. One Christmas, when I was thirteen, my Grandma Margret visited for the holidays. She took me to the Winter Park Mall to Christmas shop. Most kids my age ran straight to the arcade or food court at the mall. Not me. I made a beeline to the Foot Locker to see all the new shoes on display. I already had some Christmas money burning a hole in my pocket, and my mission was to spend every dime on fresh new kicks.

When we walked into the Foot Locker, time stopped. The most beautiful shoes I had ever seen were right before me. I didn't even know what brand of shoes they were, as I had never seen them before. I just knew that I needed them. I made my way over to the shoe wall and picked them up. I still remember how they felt in my hand. I remember the black and red colors and the beautiful red soles. They were the original Jordan 1 high-tops. I remember turning the shoe over to check the price tag, which I still do. I don't remember exactly how much they were, only the devastating realization that I didn't have enough Christmas money to buy them. I quickly put the shoe back on the display, and noticing my immediate loss of enthusiasm, my grandma asked me what was wrong. I told her I didn't have enough money for the shoes. She picked the shoe up, looked at the price tag, and said, "Let me have your money." She asked a salesperson for the shoe in my size, and they returned quickly with the precious box.

My grandma told me to sit next to her, and as the salesperson opened the box, it was as if they did it in slow motion. I'm pretty sure there was a spotlight that came on as well. I tried one shoe on, and my grandma said, "No, let's put them both on. I want to see what they both look like."

Now, the way I remember it, when I took my first walk in the shoe store in those shoes, people applauded. They stood in awe and wonderment at these fresh kicks. I felt taller, stronger, and faster, and I was damn sure I could suddenly jump higher. Grandma Margret and I walked to the register, and she made up the difference. *I had my first pair of Jordans. The love affair had begun.*

"I'm not sure what the return on investment was for an updated closet, but I know what it was when I invested in myself."

~

"This was a defining moment for me. My life slowed down that day. I realized it was time to make a change. I wasn't sure what the change would be, but I knew it would be significant."

CHAPTER TWO

Rene Rodriguez

Rene Rodriguez is a bestselling author, dynamic keynote speaker, podcast host, and someone I call my friend and mentor. This book would never have been written if our paths had not crossed. By now, you know that the "One Jordan" idea came from Rene's conversation with Brad Lea. I took his idea and took it to another level. I think it's important to share how much my life has changed since the first time I heard Rene speak. So, let me use one of the many powerful lessons Rene taught me—the importance of framing your story.

In 2021, my friend Jason Purcell attended an event called Amplifii. I did not know who Rene was. A few days after Jason returned from the event, he shared how powerful it was. My first question was, of course, "How much did it cost?" When he told me, I wasn't sure about making the financial commitment. I did what most people would do. I googled Rene Rodriguez to see what all the hype was about. That's when my RA, or reticular activating system, kicked in. And now, I am seeing Rene everywhere.

Almost every influential person I knew in the mortgage space had attended the intimate two-and-a-half-day event. I'll give you some perspective on the cost. At this point, the two days would be six times what

I had ever spent to attend a three-day event with several keynote speakers. I was the guy who bought the cheapest ticket so that I could get in the door. I didn't understand the value of VIP or investing in myself at that level. Then, a friend told me that the conferences aren't always about who speaks, but more about who you can meet that is attending.

The fall of 2021, at the Planet Hollywood Hotel in Las Vegas, would be the first time I heard Rene speak. The cost of this event was approximately $300. I used this day to determine if I wanted to invest more in Amplifii. I remember being the first person to show up and waiting for the doors to open. I am always the guy who tries to sit up front, but not for the reasons you may think. Yes, up front is nice. However, it's about paying attention and only seeing the stage and the presenters without distractions. The doors opened, and I took my seat. The room filled quickly, which should tell you something. It's Las Vegas, 8:00 a.m. The room was packed, and we started on time. This was my kind of crowd. As I looked around the room, it was like scrolling through my IG feed. Everyone I followed from the industry was there to support Rene.

Remember, this was a test run for me. Did I want to make the financial commitment to Amplifii? As Rene's commanding presence on stage overtook the room, I filled my notebook with information I had never heard before. It was like opening presents on Christmas day. At the end of the event, they offered a discounted price for all attendees who wanted to attend Amplifii. I was sold and ready to make the financial commitment. The only thing stopping me was a necessary conversation with Nicki, my wife. Any time we are going to spend money and the amount involves a comma, we have a quick discussion. Mainly because I am a spender and I like to buy nice things. She keeps me grounded. So, being the salesperson I am, I role-played how the conversation might go. We had saved money to remodel our closet, and this investment was close

2. How do you view the role of conferences, seminars, or workshops in personal growth? Have you had a transformative experience at such an event?

_____

_____

_____

3. Consider a personal story that has shaped you. How might sharing this story, as the author did with his son's story, be therapeutic or influential to others?

_____

_____

_____

4. Reflect on a situation where stepping out of your comfort zone led to significant personal growth. How did you handle the discomfort, and what did you learn?

_____

_____

_____

5. Think about a time when you had to make a tough decision regarding personal development. How did you approach this decision, and what role did support from others play?

_____

_____

_____

6. Have you ever had a defining moment that made you realize the need for change in your life? How did you respond to this realization?

_____

_____

_____

7. Discuss the importance of building relationships on your professional journey. How have your connections influenced your career or personal growth?

_____

_____

_____

8. What are your thoughts on continuous learning and being part of groups like masterminds? How can such groups contribute to ongoing personal and professional development?

_____

_____

_____

"...this is the most interesting way I've ever had anybody connect with me, and it's an amazing gift. I was waiting for the other shoe to drop."

~

"You either infect or affect everyone and every room you walk into."

CHAPTER THREE

Damon West

Damon West, the author of *The Coffee Bean*, was a guest on the *Ed Mylett* podcast in May 2022. After hearing his story, I felt a strong resonance with Damon. Here's a guy who was a Division 1 quarterback with everything going for him in life. Then, following an injury, Damon struggled with addiction and ended up leading one of the largest criminal organizations in Dallas, Texas. When you hear Damon speak, there's something about his voice that, at least for me, creates a connection. His journey is remarkable—from being a Division 1 college football player to working in the stock market and then to his battle with meth addiction. Once I heard Damon's story, I knew I needed to connect with him on a more personal level. That's when our friendship began.

I started reaching out to Damon through Instagram by DMing him. When you DM people, you often get a bot responding or an assistant. However, this was Damon responding to me. I asked him the question I've asked almost everybody in this book: *"Damon, I noticed you wear Jordans. I'm just curious: which model Jordan is your favorite?"* He responded that the Jordan 3s were his favorite and asked me about mine. I told him I preferred the 5s but liked the 3s. Then, I asked him his shoe size, and he said he wore a 10.5. Then he DM'd, *"What size do you wear?"*

I responded, *"Size 14."*

It was funny because I wasn't sure how he would respond to that message regarding his shoe size, So I left it at that and wrote, *"Damon, I'd love to send you a gift just for you being so honest and transparent about your story."* Damon sent me his information, and that afternoon, I got online, found a Jordan 3, size 10.5, and shipped the shoe off with a handwritten note.

See, Damon was one of those people that I automatically felt a connection with because he responded. Our messages back and forth were personable. The cool thing was Damon and I were going to speak on the same stage about a month and a half after our first contact. So, I continued communicating with him.

Once Damon received the shoe, I got a phone call from a number I didn't recognize, with a Texas area code. It was Damon.

"Chris, *this is the most interesting way I've ever had anybody connect with me, and it's an amazing gift. I was waiting for the other shoe to drop."*

We briefly talked, and he agreed to come on my podcast. Damon's story is powerful, detailing his journey in overcoming drug addiction and becoming a "coffee bean." (This will be explained later in this chapter.) Understand that you can affect the environment, everything around you, and everyone you touch. The battles I faced as a child and understanding drug addiction were the main topics of conversation between Damon and me. Offline, we had multiple conversations, as I've had friends who were challenged with drug addiction, and even one of their children suffered from it, following a path similar to his.

Damon is one of the most gracious people I've ever been around. He offered to get on a phone call and talk to my friend's son. He offered to talk to another friend of mine who suffered from the same type of addiction. Many people in his position don't have to do these things. He's already made it to a certain level. However, Damon does not forget where he came from. He is an incredibly resilient individual who managed to reduce a life sentence to an eight-year prison term, get out, and change the world around him.

Damon has become a friend of mine and someone I regularly reach out to. When you listen to him speaking at football programs across the country and see how he affects individuals in the audience, that's what I aspire to do at some point in my career. Damon is one of those people who always has a positive word for me. During one of our first conversations, I asked him, "What can I do for you? How can I help you?"

He replied, "Chris, tell everyone you know about the 'coffee bean' story [explained later in this chapter]. If anyone needs a speaker to uplift them, please mention my name. I'll do the same for you, brother."

I gave Damon the other shoe when we finally met in person in Charleston, South Carolina. He headed to the airport that morning to fly home, and my flight was delayed for nine hours because of a hurricane. Who do I run into at the airport? Damon West. He and I sat and just had another conversation. He talked to me about always understanding how important it was to ask for help and how important it was to follow through with everything you promised. Damon knows he received a second chance, and he's done amazing things with it—speaking to the Clemson football team, the University of Alabama, Wendy's Corporation, and major corporations nationwide. He has a story to tell and share to change people's lives. This is one of my most powerful "One Jordan" connections so far.

The coffee bean story, as told by Damon West, is a powerful metaphor for personal transformation and resilience. It revolves around a young man who is facing significant challenges in his life. He confides in his father, who offers a unique perspective on adversity.

To illustrate his point, the father takes three pots and boils them: in the first pot, he places carrots; in the second, eggs; and in the third, coffee beans. Each element reacts differently to the boiling water—the carrots soften, the eggs harden, and the coffee beans change the water itself.

The father explains that the carrots, eggs, and coffee beans each faced the same adversity—boiling water—but reacted differently. The carrot went in strong but became weak; the egg was fragile but became hard; the coffee beans were unique in that they changed the water itself.

The moral of the story is about how we choose to respond to adversity. Like the coffee bean, we have the power to transform our environment and challenges into something positive. It's a reminder that when things are at their worst, we can become our best. This story encapsulates West's journey from a life filled with challenges, including imprisonment, to becoming a motivational speaker and author, embodying the transformative power of the "coffee bean."

One of my favorite quotes from Damon is, *"You either infect or affect everyone and every room you walk into."* How powerful is that?

You know, you might not think you make an impact on people when you're around, but trust me, you do. It's a huge responsibility we carry as humans. Another thing he shared really stuck with me: "You can learn from everyone. Everyone teaches you something, either the right way or the wrong way." That's something I've really taken to heart and applied in various parts of my life. When I meet new people, I'm always on the lookout for what I can learn from them. Everyone's journey is unique, after all.

There's this fascinating story that Damon tells about a SWAT team bursting in and cuffing him. He refers to them as angels, which is pretty unusual, right? Most people wouldn't see a SWAT team that way. But he believes that "God puts angels in your life in all sorts of forms." In his case, those angels were the ones who arrested him, saving him from a darker fate on the streets with meth or worse.

Damon's amazing story of changing his life around while in prison and after his release has been an inspiration to many. Damon is referred to as the "Smuggler of Hope." The prisoners look up to him, seeing in him what they could achieve if they stay on the right path. His story really shows the impact you can have on others.

Mental Activity for Personal Growth

1. Damon emphasizes we can either "infect or affect" everyone we encounter. How do you interpret this concept, and how can you apply it to your interactions and relationships?

_____

_____

_____

2. Damon believes in the power of learning from everyone, as everyone has something to teach us. Can you think of a specific instance where you learned something valuable from an unexpected source?

_____

_____

_____

3. Damon's experience with the SWAT team led him to view them as "angels" who saved his life. Can you think of a situation in your life where something initially negative turned out to be a positive or life-changing experience?

_____

_____

_____

4. The "Smuggler of Hope" was Damon's nickname in prison. How does his story illustrate the transformative power of hope and second chances? Have you ever encountered a situation where hope played a significant role in someone's life?

_____

_____

_____

5. How does Damon West's story inspire you to think differently about your challenges and opportunities for personal growth? What lessons can you take away from his journey?

_____

_____

_____

6. In what ways do you believe Damon's message of being a "coffee bean" and transforming one's environment can apply to your life or community?

_____

_____

_____

"People will reach peak performance in sports and business when they connect their head and heart."

~

"Can you look in the mirror and say you've given your best every day?"

CHAPTER FOUR

Ben Newman

Ben Newman is one of the top Performance Coaches in the world. A lot of folks know him as this dynamo motivational speaker, but if you actually chat with him, he'll tell you straight up he's a Performance Coach. He has been a Performance Coach for sports teams and corporations and is now on the big stage. He helped the University of Alabama Crimson Tide win two national championships and multiple championships with North Dakota State. He is now the performance coach at Kansas State University, which won a Big 12 Championship in 2022.

The first time I heard about Ben Newman was on this podcast, the *MFCEO Project*, hosted by Andy Frisella. Man, the energy he brought was off the charts. I was driving to some appointment, listening to it, and his vibe made me want to just stop the car and go for a run. It's still super clear in my mind. I hit the follow button on his Instagram and started tuning into his podcast, *The Burn*. I just knew I had to connect with this guy someday.

He was the second person I sent a Jordan to. I IM'd his assistant, Monique, and asked her several questions. The first was, "What does it cost to be coached by Ben Newman one-on-one?" I knew that wasn't in my budget at the time, but I wanted to know because my goal was to have him coach me one-on-one. I told Monique she'd hear more from me. "Ben will coach me at some point. Oh, and by the way, what shoe size does Ben wear?"

Monique sent me a message a few days later, letting me know his shoe size and address. I got the Jordan 1s I knew he liked to wear. I wrote my handwritten note and sent the shoe off. His response was epic. I got this text from some number I didn't recognize; it was a St. Louis area code. It's Ben Newman! He sent me pics—one of the shoe and one of the note and said, *"Chris, you've got my attention. Let's set up a call."*

I texted back, *"Absolutely, let's do it."*

"How about December 26th at 11:00 a.m.?" And just like that, we were set.

That was like my Christmas present that year, getting on a call with Ben Newman, a guy I look up to and who was willing to have a conversation. Have you ever had one of those conversations with someone you've known your whole life? That's how Ben and I became friends. We went deep into conversation and instantly talked about goals, the strategies I had in my life, and the things I wanted to accomplish. He started coaching, asking me tough questions I should have been asking myself all along.

"Chris, if your goal is to become a top-tier coach and a top-tier podcast host, how many times a day are you telling people about that?"

Well, my answer was zero.

He asked, "How do you plan to get there if no one knows?"

Those were the powerful words I needed to hear to jump in and start working toward my goal as a top-performance coach, speaker, and podcast host. He agreed to be on my podcast, and we set that up for a few months later.

You need to understand that it's not about the money for him. The money is a byproduct of all the work. He's doing what he wants by helping people get where they want to go. Ben is one of those individuals who finds the gaps you need to fill to improve your life. He says, 'What you do today manufactures everything you want in the future. And when you talk about someone's actions, you can tell how bad they want it." That was something else that resonated with me, too. At that point, I had no problem telling people about my actions, but my actions were not on track.

Ben and I have connected several times since then, and I have completed several coaching sessions with him. He's been a key reason I wrote this book. He's the one who connected me with my publisher. He also shared with me the importance of connecting head and heart. *People will reach peak performance in sports and business when they connect their head and heart.* How powerful is that? How often have you been in a situation where you're trying to positively lead someone or help someone get to the next level, but their heart and head aren't connected? This is why this guy is the best in the business. We also discussed why athletes do so well and why people in business tend not to. He said, "Because athletes put in the work every day. That's part of what they do. It's part of their process." So why don't we, as business leaders and professionals, put in the work every day? We need to know what stops us from getting it done.

Can you look in the mirror and say you've given your best every day? One challenge I want you to take from this chapter is, at the end of the day, to look in the mirror and say, "Be honest with yourself. Have you given your best today?"

He's also showing me how to be an example in life. Ben does his "Unrequired Workout," and he's done it every day for more than 1,500 days.

The Unrequired Workout

- Reverse plank: 4 minutes 44 seconds.
- Regular plank: 4 minutes 44 seconds.
- Bodyweight squats: 4 minutes 44 seconds.
- Jumping jacks: 4 minutes 44 seconds.
- Straight pushups: 44 reps, 2 sets.
- Abs: 44 reps, 4 sets.
- Cardio burst: 4 sets, 44 reps each.
- Wall sits: 4 sets, 44 seconds each.
- Kettlebell curls: 44 reps.
- Calf raises: 4 sets, 44 reps each.

I asked him, "Ben, why do you do that? Why do you put yourself through it?"

He replied, "Chris, how can I walk into the Alabama locker room or the NFL Combine and try to give advice, help people, and try to be a leader as their performance coach if I'm not in peak physical shape?"

He had a valid point. He must lead and set the example; if not, why would anyone listen? He said, "You have to be crazy about what you want in life to accomplish it."

At the intensity level, you must bring your absolute best every day to get where you want to go. Imagine this—a guy with no experience playing football but understanding how to connect heart and head is a performance coach for a Big 12 or SEC National Championship football program. How does he do that? Ben lives by the philosophy of "the burn," where his "why" and purpose connect. Ben shared that with me, and I had to do deep dives to figure out how my "why" and purpose connected. What is my burn? I'll share my burn with you.

In 2020, my son CJ passed away after 18 hours. He was born on July 2nd and passed on the 3rd. CJ is my burn, looking at me right now as I write this book. CJ sees everything I do. That's why I put in the extra work. That's why I do the extra reps in the gym. I make the extra phone calls because he can see it. The last thing I want to do is let him down. My burn is my son, CJ. I challenge you to figure out what your burn is.

Mental Activity for Personal Growth

1. Ben Newman emphasizes the importance of connecting the head and heart for peak performance. Can you think of a time when you felt a strong connection between your goals and your passion? How did this connection drive your performance and actions?

_____

_____

_____

2. Ben compares the importance of daily work and the intensity needed to achieve success with the dedication of athletes. Do you approach your goals and ambitions with the same daily commitment and intensity level? If not, what might be holding you back?

_____

_____

_____

3. I shared my "burn" or source of motivation, which is my son, CJ. What is your "burn," the driving force that keeps you motivated and committed to your goals? What does the burn mean to you? How does it influence your daily actions and decisions?

_____

_____

_____

4. Ben believes in leading by example, as seen in his commitment to a daily workout routine. How do leaders who set a personal example inspire and influence others professionally and personally?

_____

_____

_____

5. Ben Newman's philosophy involves connecting one's "why" and purpose. Have you ever taken the time to explore your "why" and purpose in life deeply? How does having a clear understanding of your "why" impact your decision-making and actions?

_____

_____

_____

6. Reflect on a time when you faced a challenge or obstacle that required you to dig deep and find your inner motivation. What strategies or mindset shifts did you employ to overcome that challenge, and what did you learn from the experience?

_____

_____

_____

"Growing up with a limb difference in the 80s was challenging; I felt like I was alone."

~

"How many times this week did you wake up and decide not to do something just because you weren't feeling up to it?"

CHAPTER FIVE

Logan Aldridge

Logan Aldridge is a fitness trainer and motivational speaker, particularly recognized for his work as a popular instructor for Peloton, a company famous for its interactive fitness products such as stationary bicycles and treadmills. What makes Aldridge's story particularly inspiring is that he is an amputee. He was a high-level competitive wakeboarder, and at 13, he lost his arm just above the elbow in an accident. Now is a good time to mention that I was born with one arm, so Logan's story deeply resonated with me. I was born with a limb difference, missing half of my left arm. *Growing up with a limb difference in the 80s was challenging; I felt like I was alone.* I consider myself one of the original adaptive athletes. Today, through social media, Logan changes lives every day by sharing his story.

Aldridge turned his personal challenge into a source of strength and inspiration. He became involved in adaptive training, which focuses on adjusting fitness and athletic activities for people with physical impairments. His work emphasizes the idea that fitness and health are accessible to everyone, regardless of their physical conditions.

He invented the Aldridge Arm, a prosthetic that helps people with limb differences work out and lift weights more efficiently. I use his invention every time I go to the gym. Logan is a motivational speaker and a mentor to people with limb differences. As a kid, I saw a few people who were like me. Today, social media and other platforms help with that.

I had a running joke. The first time I spoke with Logan, I said, "It's cool to be talking to someone with one arm. Usually, the only other time I'm in the same room with someone with one arm is at a Def Leppard concert since the drummer from Def Leppard has one arm."

I had been DMing Logan back and forth for about a year and a half to two years before he even went to work for Peloton. I saw Logan on social media being a fitness buff like I am. I saw him doing certain moves and exercises that I wanted to learn. Logan responded instantly, and we built a friendship. Finally, after two years, give or take a couple of months, I asked Logan, "What's your shoe size?"

He responded, "Oh, man, do you make shoes?"

"No," I said, "it's just my calling card."

"I wear a size ten and a half."

So, I did what I always do. I grabbed a pair of 10.5 Jordan 1s, wrote a handwritten note, and sent them to Logan.

The story is funnier this time because when Logan opened the box, he saw one shoe but not the note. His first thought was, *Oh, man, does Chris think I'm a lower extremity amputee? He only sent one shoe?* Then he found the note and reached out. Logan was so friendly and down-to-earth. He said, "Chris, you didn't have to send me anything. I would have done a Zoom call with you, no problem."

After our first conversation, I knew there would be a friendship there. Since we first connected through DM on Instagram, Logan and I have developed an amazing friendship. When he learned I lived in Florida, he invited me to a great event he was involved in. He said, "Hey, I'm playing golf in Tampa at the National Association of One Arm Golfers. Why don't you come check it out?"

One Saturday morning, I drove to meet Logan in person. An amazing thing happened that day. I got out of the car and walked up to the greens; there, I saw over eighty golfers, all with one arm, playing golf. Seeing people with various limb differences playing golf at such a high level was unbelievable. I grabbed a golf cart and followed Logan during his round. The thing I noticed most about Logan on the course, besides being super sharply well-dressed, was his excitement as he played. If you didn't know that all the players had limb differences or were missing an arm, you would have thought it was just a bunch of people playing golf and having a great time. I followed him for nine holes, had incredible conversations, and met many others at the event.

When I interviewed Logan and talked to him about the story behind losing his arm, he never once complained. He never thought about giving up. When they stitched his arm back up, he went to football practice a couple of weeks later. Now, think about that. You lose three-quarters of your arm, but you don't give up. You get out of bed and go to football practice.

How many times this week did you wake up and decide not to do something just because you weren't feeling up to it?

I connected with Logan because he's a no-nonsense, no-excuses kind of guy, and he and I are on the same page with that. We don't let our limb differences get in the way, stop us, or slow us down. Sure, I have an excuse. Logan has an excuse. But we don't let it affect us that way. Logan has done so much work in our community (the adaptive athlete space), and he continues to grow and make things happen. I found somebody doing the stuff I wanted to do, so I reached out to him in my own special way. And that's how Logan and I became good friends. Later that year, he invited me to New York City to be on Peloton Live with him and do a workout in the studio, all because I sent "One Jordan."

Mental Activity for Personal Growth

1. How often did you wake up this week and decide not to do something because you didn't feel like it? What was your excuse today for not going to the gym or committing to another exercise activity?

_____

_____

_____

2. What was your excuse for not getting things done at work or home? What are your limiting beliefs? Are you telling yourself they're stopping you from deciding to be who you want to be or from taking consistent action?

_____

_____

_____

3. Logan Aldridge's story is one of remarkable resilience and determination after losing his arm at a young age. How does Logan's ability to overcome adversity inspire you to push through challenges in your own life?

_____

_____

_____

4. The act of sending a single Jordan became a symbol of connection for me and Logan. Have you ever used a small gesture or gift to connect with someone you admire or respect? How did that gesture impact your relationship?

_____

_____

_____

5. Logan's attitude and enthusiasm while golfing with other individuals with limb differences were remarkable. How does his positive attitude and ability to find joy in life's activities resonate with you?

_____

_____

_____

6. Logan never complained or gave up after losing his arm, even returning to football practice shortly after his accident. How can Logan's resilience inspire you to persevere when faced with setbacks or obstacles?

_____

_____

_____

7. Logan and I share a no-excuse mentality despite our limb differences. What excuses or limiting beliefs have prevented you from pursuing your goals, and how can you overcome them?

_____

_____

_____

8. Logan's work in the adaptive athlete space and commitment to helping others in the community are evident. Have you ever been inspired to give back or support a cause because of someone's actions or influence in your life? If so, how did it impact you?

_____

_____

_____

9. I sent a single Jordan to Logan, eventually leading to our friendship and collaboration. Have you ever taken a seemingly insignificant action that significantly impacted your life or relationships?

_____

_____

_____

10. Logan's invitation to Chris to join him in New York City for a Peloton Live workout demonstrates the power of meaningful connections. How has building relationships and connections with people who share your values and goals enriched your life?

_____

_____

_____

11. Reflect on a time when you faced a challenge or setback, and use Logan's story to motivate you to continue pursuing your goals, regardless of the obstacles.

_____

_____

_____

"...this path led to a stark realization when I lost my fortune as rapidly as I had made it."

~

"David's philosophy of dedicating time each day to study and reflect on time management was incredibly insightful."

CHAPTER SIX

David Meltzer

David Meltzer is a figure of resilience and transformation, qualities that deeply resonate with my own journey. Like David, I too experienced early success by my own definition, prioritizing wealth creation over family, relationships, and even my health. However, *this path led to a stark realization when I lost my fortune as rapidly as I had made it.* While my financial losses paled in comparison to David's $100 million downfall, the impact on my life was no less profound.

I found David's story particularly inspiring in our interactions and through his public speaking. His journey from financial ruin back to success wasn't just about reclaiming wealth, but a profound transformation of values and priorities. This echoed my own aspirations. David's loss and subsequent rebirth highlighted the power of resilience, self-reflection, and a values-driven approach to life and business—themes that I had begun to see as vital in my own life.

My personal connection with David began when I reached out to him on Instagram. Despite his busy schedule, David responded instantly, illustrating his incredible generosity with his time. This brief interaction led me to his assistant, Nick, who helped facilitate our connection further, a testament to David's accessibility and the efficient team he has built around him. I asked Nick for David's shoe size and, in a gesture of appreciation, sent David a pair of "One Jordan" shoes. This gesture led to a heartfelt exchange and paved the way for David to share our story during a chance meeting in Las Vegas. There, amid a crowd, David paused to highlight our unique interaction, turning it into a teaching moment for those listening.

This unexpected encounter in Las Vegas, where David took the time to share our story, was a genuine surprise and demonstrated his natural ability to foster connections and use personal stories as powerful lessons. When I later spoke with David on my podcast, his insights into time management and the balance of giving and receiving struck a chord with me. *David's philosophy of dedicating time each day to study and reflect on time management was incredibly insightful.* His approach to life, emphasizing accessibility, consistency, and a balanced give-and-take in relationships, profoundly impacted me.

David's candidness about his past mistakes and his journey towards a more mindful, value-centric life inspired me. It reinforced my decision to shift my focus towards speaking and coaching, using lessons learned from our shared experiences of loss and recovery. His method of managing time and his philosophy on human interaction are lessons I've taken to heart, providing valuable insights that have shaped my approach as a performance coach and keynote speaker.

In many ways, David Meltzer's story mirrors my own—a narrative of losing what we once thought was everything, only to discover a richer, more meaningful path. It's a testament to the idea that our greatest setbacks can sometimes lead to our most significant transformations. Through his story and my interactions with him, I've gained invaluable insights, shaping my approach to performance coaching and keynote speaking.

Ultimately, David's story, enriched by our personal interactions and his universal capacity for resilience and reinvention, is a powerful reminder of the strength we can find in adversity and the endless possibilities for transformation. His journey, paralleling my own, underscores the importance of mindset, discipline, and the pursuit of high performance grounded in a strong value system.

Mental Activity for Personal Growth

1. Think about a time when you faced a significant setback or failure. How did this experience shape your understanding of success and failure? What lessons did you learn about resilience and bouncing back?

_____

_____

_____

2. The journey highlights a transformation of values and priorities after facing financial ruin. Reflect on your current values and priorities. Are they aligned with the life you desire to lead? How might you need to shift your focus to lead a more balanced and fulfilling life?

_____

_____

_____

3. The story underscores the importance of being generous and accessible. Reflect on how you balance giving and receiving. How accessible are you to others, and how does this impact your relationships and success?

_____

_____

_____

4. There's a dedication to studying time management. Reflect on your approach to managing time. How do you ensure that your daily actions align with your long-term goals? Are there any changes you could make to manage your time more effectively?

_____

_____

_____

5. Profound mindset shifts have been experienced following significant losses. Reflect on your own mindset. Have you experienced any significant shifts in how you view challenges, success, or failure? What prompted these changes?

_____

_____

_____

6. The narrative illustrates the power of human connection through personal stories. Reflect on a time when a simple act of kindness or connection had a significant impact on you or someone else. What does this story teach you about the impact of small gestures?

_____

_____

_____

7. Inspiration is found in the journeys and teachings of mentors. Reflect on the role of mentorship and storytelling in your life. Who are your mentors, and what stories have inspired you to change or grow?

_____

_____

_____

8. After significant losses, there's a redefinition of what success means. How do you define success? Has your definition changed over time? What experiences have influenced this definition?

_____

_____

_____

"...this persona of a giant man came out, commanding the stage, even though he's probably only 5'8"."

~

"If you're not reaching your full potential, the likelihood of your child doing so is slim."

CHAPTER SEVEN

Coach Michael Burt

Coach Michael Burt is one of the most passionate speakers I have encountered, transitioning from a former basketball coach to a motivational speaker and business coach. He is renowned for his "Monster Producing" approach, which combines sports coaching strategies with business and life coaching. This unique blend helps individuals and organizations unlock their potential and achieve significant growth. Burt is also an author known for his dynamic style and focus on developing a strong "coach's mindset" for success in various aspects of life. His approach, integrating sports tactics with practical coaching, inspires personal and professional growth, creating a practice that I deeply admire.

I first encountered Coach Burt at a conference in Phoenix, Arizona. I had heard his name before and seen him on social media, but I wasn't sure who he was. Then, *this persona of a giant man came out, commanding the stage, even though he's probably only 5'8".* He captivated the audience and was dressed to the nines; his ability to articulate the English language and how he grabbed hold of you were phenomenal. So, he instantly had my attention. Coach Burt will tell you he's super passionate when he gets on stage. He's going to sweat. He said, "Don't call 911 because I'm fine." The thing about Coach Burt is when he connects with you, you feel like you are the only person in the room. I was in a room of 1,000 people, and I thought he was speaking directly to me. So, at that point, I knew I had to connect with Coach Burt.

My coworker, who had been coached by Michael Burt one-on-one, helped me reach out to Coach Burt in my now familiar way. Knowing his preference for Jordans, I sent him a pair of Jordan 1s. "I'm Coach Burt. I got the shoe and the letter," he responded. His reaction to this unconventional introduction was enlightening. "I get a lot of things from people; some of them are cool, and some are just notes. But my wife told me, 'Hey, you must check this one out.'" His daughter's reaction upon finding one shoe and a note in the box was a moment of curiosity and surprise for him.

Coach Burt believes in remarkable boldness and rewards people for taking the initiative. He called me and said, "I'm rewarding you for being bold. I believe in creativity. There's a shortage of initiative in the world, and you took the initiative to reach out and contact me." That was like hitting a home run. I was on a phone call with Coach Michael Burt, a guy I look up to, who is an inspiration in the coaching world and a Jordan fan. We had a quick conversation, and he agreed to be on my podcast. Not only that, but he also agreed to do a 45-minute call with my team and staff to review his new book, Flip the Switch. This high-level individual was willing to take a couple of hours out of his day because I sent "One Jordan."

One of the biggest takeaways I got from Coach Burt was something he calls "Prey Drive." This concept, inspired by a story from a Vietnam vet, resonates deeply with my philosophy. Coach Burt's eloquent and intentional use of words taught me that "prey drive" in humans is the ability to see something and pursue it passionately.

Coach Burt shared with me a story about potential that really hit home. He was coaching a girls' basketball team and often had parents approach him, proudly saying, "My daughter has so much potential." Coach Burt's response was insightful. He'd say, "But is your kid seeing you reach your full potential? Because the things our kids see are caught, not taught." He was very clear with the parents: *"If you're not reaching your full potential, the likelihood of your child doing so is slim."*

In essence, Coach Burt highlighted the critical role parents play as role models. He believed that for these young athletes to truly tap into their potential, they needed to see their parents actively pursuing and fulfilling their own dreams and ambitions. This approach, he argued, would set a powerful example for the children, showing them the importance and reality of reaching their full potential.

Coach Burt's story and his teachings are essential to understanding the power of continuous growth, passion, and relentless pursuit of excellence. His journey and the impact he has had on both individuals and organizations exemplify the transformative potential of effective coaching and leadership. His influence on me has been profound, shaping my approach to coaching and personal development. Coach Burt's story is a vital part of this book, illuminating the pathways to unlocking true potential in ourselves and inspiring it in others.

Mental Activity for Personal Growth

1. Coach Michael Burt's ability to captivate an audience with his passion and articulation was highlighted throughout this chapter. Have you ever experienced a speaker or presenter who had a similar impact on you? What qualities or characteristics do you believe make a speaker genuinely effective?

_____

_____

_____

2. Coach Burt's willingness to reward boldness and initiative resonates with everyone he meets. How can recognizing and rewarding bold actions positively impact individuals and organizations? Have you encountered similar situations where boldness was rewarded?

_____

_____

_____

3. The concept of "Prey Drive" is introduced as a critical concept by Coach Burt. How do you interpret the concept of "Prey Drive"?

_____

_____

_____

4. How can the concept of "Prey Drive" help you maintain your motivation and drive when faced with long-term challenges or setbacks? Are there strategies or habits you employ to stay focused on your goals?

_____

_____

_____

5. Coach Burt seeks to activate "Prey Drive," even as he faces the later stages of his coaching career. How do you stay motivated and continue to pursue excellence in your career or personal endeavors as time passes? Are there new strategies or sources of inspiration you can explore?

_____

_____

_____

6. Coach Burt's proactive approach to trademarking "Prey Drive" demonstrates his ability to seize opportunities. Have you ever identified an opportunity and taken bold action to pursue it? What was the result, and how did it impact your life or career?

_____

_____

_____

7. Reflect on the idea of "flipping the switch" in your life. Can you identify moments or strategies when you consciously activated your motivation and drive to achieve a goal or overcome an obstacle? What triggers or actions have worked for you in the past?

_____

_____

_____

8. Coach Burt's reflection on potential and the importance of parents setting an example for their children is significant. How do your actions and behaviors as a parent or role model influence the potential and aspirations of the younger generation? Can you think of specific ways to lead by example?

_____

_____

_____

"He's doing the work, being good to people, building his team, keeping his word, and recreating and reinventing himself daily."

~

"We are in the era of the worst leader in history. It's embarrassing."

CHAPTER EIGHT

Andy Elliot

Andy Elliott is a prominent figure in sales training, particularly automotive sales. Born in 1980 in the United States, Elliott started his professional career as a car salesperson at 18. Over time, he excelled in this field, setting records for the most money made by a car salesperson in a single month and year. His success in sales led him to establish The Elliott Group in September 2010, a company that provides sales training to more than 11,000 companies and 600,000 salespeople across 176 countries.

As you've learned by this point, I'm intrigued by successful people. Although car sales wasn't a passion of mine, the opportunity to spend time with someone with such an amazing success story continues to intrigue me. So, when I learned of Andy's successful rise, I sent him my signature introduction gift—"One Jordan." A few days later, I received a text and video from Ian Macklin, Andy's VP of sales and development, and Andy himself, stating we would set up a call soon.

After some aggressive follow-up on my end, the kind a good car guy would respect, Ian put me in touch with Marielle, the best assistant on the planet. She was in charge of Andy's schedule, a monumental task. If you see him on Instagram, you know how busy he is. Marielle scheduled a time for Andy and me to connect. The call was scheduled, and to say I was excited was an understatement.

I was nervous on the day of the call, unsure if I could match his intensity. Seeing someone every day who's always bringing it can be intimidating. My wife said, "Be yourself and enjoy the call." I'm excited to share with you the call I had with Andy.

He started the call with his nine-figure smile, and I was instantly calmed and ready to talk. Every day, Andy says his mind is blown. The growth of his company has been off the charts. He's aligned himself with other super-high producers, like world-famous entrepreneur, author, and YouTuber Patrick Bet-David, who talks about compressing time.

Let me expand on this theory for you. Bet-David emphasizes that by maximizing efficiency and focusing on what truly matters, individuals and businesses can achieve their long-term goals at an accelerated pace. This involves strategic planning, ruthless prioritization, and the elimination of distractions or unproductive activities. By doing so, one can make the most of every hour, leading to significant achievements over a shorter period.

Bet-David's approach goes beyond traditional productivity tips. It's about a mindset shift—viewing time as a precious commodity and aligning every action towards the most impactful outcomes. This philosophy resonates particularly well with entrepreneurs and business leaders who operate in fast-paced environments where the cost of time is high.

Andy has put this concept into practice. Many people might not believe it's real, but it's been authentic for Andy. He said, "Anybody who knows something you don't will cost you money by not knowing what they know or do." He spends most of his time learning, growing, and practicing his craft. He then implements what he learns in his life and teaches it in the classroom.

This type of growth would be impossible without a team. Andy said, "This is why most people don't succeed or crush their goals." When you see Andy at an event or on social media, you see his team—the Elliot Army. Andy is known for not only paying his people very well but also treating them even better. He mentioned on social media the other day that people can't recruit his team because of how well he takes care of them and treats them. Social media is a huge part of Andy's success.

At the time of writing this book, Andy had 649,000 followers on Instagram under the official Andy Elliot account, 175,000 on Facebook, 448,000 on YouTube, and 328,000 on TikTok. He felt like it took a long time to build that out. He said, "Anytime you're building something like that, it's going in slow motion."

Here's one of the most exciting stats I've ever heard: Today, the Elliot Army averages 150 million views every 28 days on their video content. "God is good," said Andy. *He's doing the work, being good to people, building his team, keeping his word, and recreating and reinventing himself daily.*

I always wonder what's going on behind the scenes when we see people out there killing it and dominating the marketplace. What work did it take to get there? How are you able to push through and grow at that rapid pace? I told Andy I stepped away from my corporate job to focus on coaching.

"There's such a huge gap between leaders and salespeople in this country," I stressed. "I feel the CEO has a hard time communicating with the salespeople. Until we help someone fill that gap, tensions will always exist. There will always be stress on those salespeople and tons of turnover."

Andy added, "*We are in the era of the worst leader in history. It's embarrassing.* This is a huge opportunity, Chris, for people like us. It's never been easier to win."

Fitness is a very important part of his lifestyle. Being fit is a requirement to be in the Elliot Army. I asked Andy when it became a part of his lifestyle, and he said, "One day, his wife grabbed his love handle and said, 'Somebody is getting a little comfortable.'" You could tell by his response that he was disappointed when that was said to him. "This really made me upset." He went to war with himself that day. Once he started getting in shape, it made him dangerous and fast. He learned that being fit and healthy would almost be a catalyst for him and his business to help catapult him to another level.

You'll kill it in business if you are physically in good condition and mentally strong. This became a core value of the Elliot Army. When Andy coached people and taught his team mindset, sales skills, and leadership, he found that the people who were the most fit had the best results. That's when he opened his fitness division of the L.A.N. Army, and now has a trainer to the stars, Aaron Williamson, as part of that group.

Andy said, "The fit person will always outperform the person who is out of shape." You'll see what I'm talking about when you see the Elliot Army. They look like a physical army. They're all specimens. They've all worked to be in the best shape to outperform the competition, which is what they're doing as they take over the sales training industry.

Andy doesn't want to be like anyone else. He shared a story about when he started doing group workouts the night before his world-famous Master Closer seminar. People told him he was crazy for doing this. He said he would get all the people out there, and they would throw heavy sandbags, do kettlebell swings, work out, and sweat together.

Andy believes exercising is why a thousand people attend his monthly event. Imagine that: a thousand people a month traveling to attend an event, gathering in a room, or outside working out. The energy must be amazing.

"You're never going to earn out your self-worth," he said. "If you don't think you're worth it, it won't happen. Being in the gym daily helps you grow your self-confidence and increases your self-worth." It's also his personal therapy.

I agree with that a thousand percent. Working out keeps me focused and helps me stack my wins throughout the day. When I start my day with a super-aggressive workout, I know there's not much that can be thrown at me afterward that would throw me off or take me off course. Andy surrounds himself with just a few people as far as top producers he likes to hang out and spend time with. The first was Rob Bailey, the musician. Then there's Bradley, known as the "Real Bradley," a massive entrepreneur; Keaton Hoskins, known as "The Muscle" from Limitless Society; and Patrick Bet-David (who I mentioned earlier). "These are all my brothers now," said Andy. They've gone from being mentors to a brotherhood.

These are the people he spends most of his time with. So, my question is, who are you spending your time with? Are you putting yourself in rooms where maybe you felt you didn't belong at one point? This is a perfect example of taking action and turning it into something to help fulfill your dreams.

When you look at the massive impact that Andy Elliot and the Elliot Army have, you realize this isn't luck. It's hard work, a dialed-in strategy, understanding where you want to go, and having massive support from your core group around you. When you talk to Andy, you'll find he's one of the kindest people you can converse with, but he's incredibly intimidating when you see him on video. I believe that's how he lives his lifestyle. He pushes himself and brings everyone else around him up to that level or standard, takes no excuses, and goes after it.

He's also kind. Andy said, "The greatest advice anyone can receive is to out-self-develop everyone in their space." What most people do is learn just enough to earn the bare minimum, and then they slow down. They read just enough books to have enough conversations to make enough money and then slow down. So, never stop self-developing and never slow down. It's the greatest advice anyone could ever receive. Oh, yeah, he added, "And hit the gym daily."

Connecting with Andy has been an amazing opportunity. He responded to "One Jordan" and was kind enough to jump on a call with me, which became an episode on my podcast. This is just another story or proof that when you find the people you want to connect with, there's always a way to do it.

Mental Activity for Personal Growth

1. Andy Elliot's emphasis on learning, growing, and practicing his craft resonates throughout this chapter. How do you approach your own personal and professional development? Are there specific strategies or habits you employ to improve yourself?

_____

_____

_____

2. The concept of "compressing time" is mentioned. How do you interpret the idea of compressing time, and how can it be applied to accelerate your progress in various areas of life?

_____

_____

_____

3. I talk a lot about Andy's social media presence and the impact of the Elliot Army. How do you perceive the role of social media in personal branding and business growth today? Have you encountered examples where a robust online presence has significantly benefited someone's career or business?

_____

_____

_____

4. The importance of physical fitness and mental strength is highlighted in this chapter. How do you prioritize your health and well-being in your daily life? Have you noticed a correlation between physical fitness and performance in other areas, such as work or personal relationships?

_____

_____

_____

5. Andy's mindset and commitment to self-improvement are evident. What are your personal beliefs about self-worth and self-confidence? Do you agree that investing in yourself, whether through fitness or other means, can positively impact your self-esteem and overall success?

_____

_____

_____

6. The importance of the company you keep is discussed. Reflect on your network and the people you surround yourself with. Are you intentionally seeking mentors and peers who inspire and challenge you to grow? How has your network influenced your personal and professional development?

_____

_____

_____

7. The story of Andy's group workout before his Master Closer seminar is shared as an example of his unique approach. Can you recall situations where taking unconventional actions paid off for you personally or professionally? What lessons did you learn from those experiences?

_____

_____

_____

8. Andy's perspective on self-worth and its relationship with income is mentioned. How do you perceive the connection between self-worth and financial success in your own life? Do you believe that personal self-worth is critical to achieving financial goals?

_____

_____

_____

9. The chapter concluded by mentioning the importance of surrounding oneself with the right people. Are there individuals or groups in your life that you consider your "brothers" or a close-knit community? How has the support of such individuals influenced your journey and achievements?

_____

_____

_____

10. Reflect on your goals and aspirations. Are there areas where you could benefit from a mentor, a community, or a fitness regimen to support your growth and progress? How can you take action to align

yourself with the right people and resources to accelerate your journey?

_____

_____

_____

"When you're a salesperson, your job doesn't start until someone says no."

~

"Dan shared ABR, which stands for 'Always Be Recording.' He showed me a camera off to the side of his desk where he records everything."

CHAPTER 9

Dan Martell

Dan Martell is an entrepreneur, bestselling author, speaker, coach, and someone who is exactly who he says he is. What do I mean by that? I heard about him when he was a guest on *The Burn* with Ben Newman. I sat in the sauna listening to the episode. I was using this episode to pass the time, trying to keep my mind off how hot 160 degrees was for 25 minutes. Dan talked about his book, *Buy Back Your Time,* and I felt as if he spoke directly to me. I ordered the book from Amazon while sitting in the sauna. When I returned home, I shared the episode with my wife. I listen to many podcasts and rarely hear something I can't wait to share with her.

The next day, when the book arrived, I started reading it immediately. Let me give you a little perspective. I have purchased a lot of books, probably too many, just as I do new Jordans. Usually, the new books I buy go into my waiting-to-read stack. However, this book moved to the front of the line. With a highlighter in hand and ready to use the C.A.T. method (change, apply, teach), I went to work highlighting everything I wanted to remember and share with anyone who would listen. During our ILC group coaching call, I shared the book and podcast. My mind was made up. Dan would be added to the "One Jordan" list. Sending him a Jordan and having him on the *One Hand At A Time* Podcast was a must. I sent Dan a DM, and he asked me to connect with his assistant. This is very common when trying to connect with high-profile individuals. Unfortunately, they declined the offer to be a guest on my show. No worries. *When you're a salesperson, your job doesn't start until someone says no.*

My coach, Adam, enjoyed the book so much that he connected with Dan and signed up to be coached with him. I thought that was my way to get Dan's shoe size. I would use (up to this point) my signature undefeated "One Jordan" strategy. Adam texted me his shoe size, and a single Jordan shoe was immediately on the way. Dan's assistant reached out and asked for my address; he wasn't interested in having a meeting.

A few days later, I received the shoe and the note back. This was the first time my signature "One Jordan" method was rejected. I was offended, and I let my ego take over. *Why would someone turn this down? Who does that? Don't you remember where you came from?* These were the thoughts that played repeatedly in my head. I felt defeated by the rejection and thought, *I should give up and move on.*

After gaining clarity and realizing that if I wanted to connect with Dan, the only things that could stop me were myself or a restraining order, I thought, *How can I make this connection happen?* I leaned on Adam, my coach, who was going to see Dan in person soon. Adam said he would talk to Dan, and it worked. Dan agreed to give me 15 minutes of his time.

I share this with you for two reasons. First, don't take no for an answer if you really want something. The other reason is that Dan lived up to who he says he is. There was no denying that. He valued his time and didn't share it with just anybody. My ego almost cost me this chapter. How many times has your ego cost you something in your life?

Dan started the call by saying he had checked out my Instagram and loved my motivation and hustle. That's a perfect example of your social media being your digital resume. Your resume can open or close doors, and remember, content is king. If you don't follow Dan, grab your phone and follow him on IG @danmartell. He posts multiple times a day, giving you proven tactics for free. Dan started sharing on social media as a blogger in 2006; yes, that's 17 years ago. He talks about social media as a muscle you must train daily. Consistency is key for social media. Dan says IG is the best platform for selling in your DMs. You must set up your profile correctly. He prefers text messaging on the site over voice messaging. The only time to use voice messages is to prove you are human and not a bot.

I asked Dan how many platforms he used. I had recently attended a conference where the presenters talked about the seven different social media platforms people use. Most people post on six platforms daily, which sounded like quite a bit. Dan stated he posted on all platforms. He has an eight-figure coaching business and a social media team that costs him over a million dollars a year. He reiterated that the best thing for someone like me, or someone starting out, was to focus on posting to Instagram. "Go all in on Instagram," he said, "consistency is key."

I was curious about what he meant by "consistency is the key."

He explained, "If you're looking to hire a coach and you're looking at ten different people on social media, and someone is showing up every day, while others are inconsistent, who would you choose as a coach?" When you see someone post every day or occasionally, you know what you'll get on the coaching side. Behaviors don't change, just as a zebra doesn't change its stripes. *Dan shared ABR, which stands for "Always Be Recording." He showed me a camera off to the side of his desk where he records everything.* I do something similar. I call it the dime cam. I have it off to the side during my coaching sessions, and I hit a button to record things I want to turn into reels or chop up later. He's a little more detailed than me. Dan's camera recordings are downloaded immediately to a Dropbox once his sessions end, and his team turns them into reels, posting up to three times a day on his social media. They post other things from more speaking events or shoot reels, but most content comes from his camera on the side.

After our chat, I picked up a copy of Dan's book *Buy Back Your Time: Get Unstuck, Reclaim Your Freedom, and Build Your Empire.* Here are a few key takeaways. DoD is the "definition of done," probably the most valuable thing I read in the book. Those of us who have kids know this very well. When we ask a child to clean their room, their "definition of done" often differs from ours. This is no different from dealing with someone in the workplace. When you communicate your expectations, define your parameters, and clarify that you need a task completed according to specific standards, you're essentially guiding them toward understanding your "definition of done." The job will get completed and be much clearer for those with clear expectations. Imagine how much time can be saved. Buy back your time by engaging in a decisive conversation with someone where you're super clear about what and how you want the task completed.

My next move was to figure out a way to get Dan on my podcast. Hopefully, he'll read the copy of this book I plan on sending him and decide it's a good time to come on. Toward the end of our conversation, I told Dan we'd share a stage at some point and be able to have more detailed conversations, and he said he looked forward to it. Dan also advised me, "Just keep giving Chris. If you continue to give through social media and be the best coach you can, your business will not fail; it will continue to grow." Great advice. He also said, "We're here to do two things: be the best version of ourselves every day and share that with everyone, and heal ourselves and help others heal themselves."

Mental Activity for Personal Growth

1. How do you prioritize and value your time, and what strategies could you adopt from Dan Martell's approach to improve your time management?

_____

_____

_____

2. Reflect on your social media presence. How does it represent you as a professional or individual, and what changes might you consider aligning it more closely with your goals?

_____

_____

_____

3. How important do you think consistency is in content creation and personal branding? Do you have a strategy for maintaining consistency in your content creation?

_____

_____

_____

4. Dan Martell emphasizes the practice of recording sessions and reflecting on them. How can this practice benefit your personal development or professional endeavors?

_____

_____

_____

5. Reflect on the concept of the "definition of done," as explained by Dan. How can clearer communication of expectations enhance productivity and clarity in your work or personal life?

_____

_____

_____

"Failure is the most critical ingredient in building success."

~

"Stop living a life by circumstance and start living a life by design."

CHAPTER TEN

Clinton Sparks

When you google "Who is Clinton Sparks?" you'll discover he's an American DJ and record producer. That description doesn't even scratch the surface of who he is. Scrolling through his *Wikipedia* page, you will see an impressive list of accomplishments and the artists he has worked with. The list is so long I would need to add another chapter to share them all. So, I will tell you my favorites: P. Diddy, Pitbull, Jo Jo, Jermaine Dupree, Lady Gaga, and Teddy Riley. Clinton has sold over eighty million records in his career and is a giant in the music industry and beyond. Most people would have stopped there, but Clinton wanted to share everything he had learned and help others learn from his experience. He released his first book, *How to Win Big in the Music Business*, and gave it away for free. Clinton didn't look at his book as an opportunity to make money but an opportunity to help others.

In October 2023, I attended an amazing event in Dallas, Texas. The event was called AMPCON, which was Rene Rodriguez's annual event. That name might sound familiar if you read the foreword and introduction to this book. If you skipped it like most of us do, please go back and read it now.

The night before the event started, I was at the VIP dinner. By this point, I'm sure, or at least I hope you know, I enjoy being in rooms where I do not yet belong. On the flight to Dallas, I listened to a podcast episode where Rene interviewed Clinton Sparks. I knew Clinton was someone I wanted to talk to if the opportunity presented itself. I saw Clinton's friendliness as I had dinner a few tables away. Even though I knew I wanted to meet him, my self-doubt kicked in. *Why would he want to talk to me?* This is a conversation I have with myself whenever I meet someone new.

I determined Clinton was approachable by the conversations I observed he had with everyone in the room. Then, I saw Clinton wearing Jordan 1s and knew that would be my icebreaker. I was wearing a pair of Jordan 1s as well. We had a great conversation; he asked me about me. What?! Clinton Sparks asked Chris Welton about Chris Welton. It didn't get much better than that for me.

I shared my book cover and the story behind it. Clinton said it was a dope cover and a dope idea. The Jordan connection continues. The next day at the conference, Clinton was on stage speaking. I took pages of notes and knew I had to send him "One Jordan." When he received the single shoe, Clinton texted me and said he would be happy to jump on a Zoom with me; he even offered to do it the same day. I was blown away by Clinton's generosity with his time. When we hopped on the call the next day, I asked Clinton, "What was the greatest lesson he had ever learned?" His first response was there were way too many lessons to share, but the most powerful lesson he ever learned was not to burn bridges. Far too many people burn bridges and shoot themselves in the foot because they don't treat others respectfully or as kindly as they should. Too often, they use people to help them accomplish what they want and then move on. Clinton said the key is to treat everyone with kindness. Don't focus on what they can do for you; instead, focus on what you can do for them, and it will come back to you. He said he couldn't count the number of times people five or even ten years later remembered how he treated them and can now do the same or even help him.

Recently, a person he helped connected him with *Entrepreneur* magazine, and from that introduction, Clinton became a writer and partner of the magazine. He could share hundreds of these types of stories. Always leave a trail of goodness behind you. It will always come back to you.

Clinton is incredibly genuine and has been working in self-development for some time. When I asked for his thoughts on the current self-development space, he said, "Too many people are getting on stages and acting like they have it all figured out. There are too many 'Johnny-come-latelies' who become life coaches and self-proclaimed gurus, regurgitating other people's content and wisdom, pretending it's their own."

He clarified that it's okay to use information you've learned from others, but you need to give them credit. "You must pay attention to the message, not the messenger. Not everybody is for everybody. It's okay to listen to someone if they are an expert in the topic you need help with, but please figure that out for yourself. Don't follow them just because everyone else does," he advised.

I asked Clinton what he's learning now. He shared that he's learning to be a good, caring, communicative CEO. He has been a hustler all his life, always juggling multiple things at once and rarely saying no. For most of his business career, Clinton has been the number two or three person in companies. Now, he is the CEO of his new endeavor.

Over the years, he has learned how to run a company and treat people, and perhaps more importantly, how not to run a company and how not to treat people. He has created a unique recipe for winning by combining this knowledge with everything he has become as a human and a leader. This recipe was perfected by seeking advice from people who have done what he is aiming to do. The most essential ingredient, he found, was surrounding himself with the right people.

I asked Clinton how failure had shaped his life. *"Failure is the most critical ingredient in building success,"* he said. Understanding failure, he believes, is the path to understanding success. "When you see how people have failed, whether as a parent, friend, or leader of a company, you get to see what they did wrong and how they fixed it. That's where you learn the most from failure."

Today, many people want to copy other successful people and mimic their actions. According to him, "That's the quickest way to lose." Avoiding mistakes, and particularly avoiding failure, often means evading success. Coming up in the industry, Clinton would look at those he considered great and analyze what they did wrong or what he thought they were forgetting to do. He honed in on that weakness and became great at it. He made it his strength. It's easy to see how to be great, but not easy to live it. You must persevere, scale, and put aside your emotions, greed, and ego.

As the interview continued, Clinton made a compelling argument about listening to others and denying the need to be always right. In today's world, we spend too much time talking and not listening. Really listening. How can we be great humans or leaders without listening? Being open to changing your mind is a powerful tool. Just because someone else has a different perspective does not mean they are wrong. Clinton explained, "It might not work for you, but it is not a reason to fight or argue." Open communication about how we think and feel can solve most problems in both personal and professional relationships.

Ask yourself this one question. How many times have you not communicated with someone you disagree with, and it resulted in the loss of a friend, family member, or business deal? Being stubborn and letting your ego get in the way will destroy relationships. I want you to understand this is not wishful thinking. Please stop being narrow-minded and realize there are more people in the world than just you. We all deserve to be heard.

Clinton has an incredible perspective on overcoming the tragedies of our past. It's important to understand that this isn't something he read or heard on a podcast. He was abandoned by an alcoholic father and is a survivor of sexual abuse and severe bullying as a kid. He has also been broke and was even arrested in his youth.

Fortunately, Clinton said, "It's not a long road. It's a decision only you can make that this stuff is not going to bother you anymore. You must start building the life you want. *Stop living a life by circumstance and start living a life by design.*"

Mental Activity for Personal Growth

1. Considering Clinton's decision to give away his book for free, what is his approach to success and mentorship? How does this reflect on the importance of knowledge sharing in professional growth?

_____

_____

_____

2. Clinton emphasizes the importance of treating everyone with kindness and not burning bridges. How can this principle be applied in your own professional or personal life?

_____

_____

_____

3. Clinton discusses the issue with self-proclaimed gurus in the self-development space. How does this perspective challenge the current state of the self-help and motivational industry?

_____

_____

_____

4. Clinton sees failure as a crucial ingredient for success. Reflect on a personal experience of failure and how it contributed to your growth or understanding of success.

_____

_____

_____

5. Based on Clinton's views on listening and being open to changing your mind, how do you think effective communication can impact leadership and personal relationships?

_____

_____

_____

6. Clinton has overcome significant personal challenges in his life. How does his story inspire resilience and the ability to design one's life despite past tragedies?

_____

_____

_____

"Welton, are you taking this all in? This will be your green room, too, someday."

~

"When he was writing the book, he said he was in tune with God's highest frequency."

CHAPTER ELEVEN

Jon Gordon

Jon Gordon is a bestselling author and keynote speaker best known for his book *The Energy Bus: 10 Rules to Fuel Your Life, Work, and Team with Positive Energy*. Jon is a friend and mentor to Damon West and Ben Newman, whom you might recognize from the previous chapters. Ben connected me with Jon and provided me with his shoe size.

I sent Jon "One Jordan" and waited for his response, and after a few weeks, I reached out to Ben to ensure Jon had received it. Ben said he received the Jordan but was busy as it was training camp for college football and the NFL. Jon works for several teams and spends most of the pre-season bouncing from city to city. I DM'd Jon a few times, and he was very responsive. He told me he had received the single shoe and would connect once training camp was over. At this point, I doubted we could connect in time to get this chapter in the book.

Then something unexpected happened: Ben Newman, who knew I was from Orlando, invited me to a charity event where he and Jon Gordon were speaking. This and the Dan Martell experience prove that the "One Jordan" invitation doesn't always lead to the results I hope for; sometimes, I need to do more. I was uncertain about how to connect with Jon at the event. Fortunately, I was meeting Ben for an early workout the morning before he spoke. During our workout, Ben kindly offered for me to walk over to the event with him. We went together, and to my surprise, Ben was able to get me a backstage VIP pass. This felt like the perfect opportunity to finally meet Jon.

I remember standing in the green room, taking it all in. Ben approached me and said, "Welton, are you taking this all in? This will be your green room, too, someday." Moments later, Jon entered. I waited patiently and then walked over to him and introduced myself.

At first, he seemed a little caught off guard. I showed him the book cover, and it clicked. Jon said, "Oh, you're the Jordan guy." He was so impressed by the book cover he had me share it with a few others backstage. I then asked Jon for a 15-minute phone call, and he agreed to do it in a few weeks. Of course, the closer in me tried to schedule a face-to-face Zoom call for my podcast; unfortunately, his schedule would not allow it.

"Maybe we can do a podcast swap after this book is a bestseller," I asked. "What do you think, Jon?" He said when things slowed down, he would. Let me give you some perspective. He lectured every day, sometimes even twice a day, so slowing down meant he was only speaking every other day. "I can't imagine how busy your schedule is and how hard it is to manage your schedule when you're speaking that often," I said.

On the day of our call, Jon was driving back from San Diego to Los Angeles. Everything happened as agreed, and he allowed me to record the phone call so I could share the conversation as a chapter in this book. I asked Jon, "How do you keep up with everything?"

"You have to have a team," he said—the obvious answer from the fifteen-time best-selling author who focuses on, you guessed it, teamwork.

Jon has a team that supports him by managing his calendar, travel, emails, speaking engagements, and time management. Most entrepreneurs have trouble handing over the reins to their teams, which is why they fail to scale their businesses. Building a team around you and trusting whom you can delegate to is essential to success.

I asked, "What should I do to get more speaking opportunities?"

His answer was straightforward. "If you want to speak more, speak more. Speak anywhere and everywhere. Then, you'll be referred and get more opportunities to speak. Some talks might be small, but it's all about putting in the reps. This will prepare you for the big stage. If you have a book you've written, send a picture of the cover to a group you'd like to speak to and say, 'I'd like to help you with this.' When you do this, people will continue to refer you, which is how you will grow. Be active on social media, not just posting but also commenting on other people's posts and sending/responding to direct messages."

One of the main reasons I wanted to connect with Jon was to figure out how he built his relationships with college and professional sports teams. Jon's first talk to a professional team was with the NFL's Jacksonville Jaguars. The coach at the time, Jack Del Rio, read Jon's book *Energy Bus*, which positively impacted him. Jack reached out to Jon and asked him if he would be interested in coming to speak to the team. Jon, of course, accepted. After that, it took off with referrals to the Atlanta Falcons, and the Universities of Texas, Georgia, and Clemson. He didn't solicit these teams; they called him. This is when you know it's your calling.

I told Jon about the "One Jordan" list I had made and why he was on it. I also told him how much *The Energy Bus* positively impacted my life. I truly respect Jon for being the person he portrays in his books. Jon shared with me that *The Energy Bus* represents the best of him, and he spends his life striving to live up to it. *When he was writing the book, he said he was in tune with God's highest frequency.*

During our conversation, I asked Jon, "Do you ever feel like you're not enough? Do you ever ask yourself, 'Why do people listen to me?'"

Jon's answer was a simple "Yes."

He said he used to ask himself, *Why would people listen to me, and why am I talking to this crowd onstage?* But not anymore. Every morning, Jon goes on what he calls a gratitude walk. He walks and prays, saying, "I am worthy, God, not in myself, but in you." Now, it's like a conviction. He does what he is supposed to be doing. He still gets nervous occasionally but has a higher level of confidence and conviction.

Jon knows why he is here and what he is doing. This part of the conversation reminds me, and I hope it reminds you as well, that every person in this book I had the privilege of interviewing is just that—a person. They are like you and me, and you and I are capable of everything they do, if we're willing to do the work.

Mental Activity for Personal Growth

1. Considering Jon Gordon's emphasis on having a team, how can teamwork be applied in various aspects of personal and professional life? Reflect on an experience where teamwork played a crucial role in your success.

_____

_____

_____

2. Jon advises that if you want to speak more, start by speaking anywhere and everywhere. How does this approach to growth and exposure resonate with your own experiences or aspirations?

_____

_____

_____

3. The book _The Energy Bus has_ significantly impacted many, including professional teams. What makes a message resonate so strongly across diverse audiences, and how can this apply to your communication strategies?

_____

_____

_____

4. Jon admits to feelings of inadequacy despite his success. How does acknowledging and confronting self-doubt contribute to personal and professional growth? Can you relate to these feelings in your journey?

_____

_____

_____

5. Jon goes on a daily gratitude walk, affirming his worthiness. How can practices like gratitude walks and affirmations impact one's mindset and performance?

_____

_____

_____

6. Jon's success with teams began with one opportunity that led to many referrals. How important are personal branding and networking in creating opportunities, and how can you apply this to your career or personal goals?

_____

_____

_____

7. Jon strives to live up to the ideals he presents in his books. How does authenticity in one's professional life affect their impact and success? Reflect on a time when being authentic significantly impacted your life.

_____

_____

_____

8. Jon's initial feelings of "Why would people listen to me?" reflect a common phenomenon known as imposter syndrome. Recognizing and addressing imposter syndrome can significantly aid in personal development and achieving success.

_____

_____

_____

"Everything we are told and taught is wrong."

~

"If it weren't for failure, we would have zero success."

CHAPTER TWELVE

Tarek El Moussa

Most of you might recognize Tarek El Moussa from his long-running mega-hit reality TV show on HGTV, *Flip or Flop*. He is also an incredible real estate investor. The show, which started in 2013, showcases the business of renovating distressed properties for profit. Tarek ventured into real estate at an early age, obtaining his license at 21 and eventually shifting from being an agent to house flipping.

Besides *Flip or Flop*, Tarek has a successful real estate agency in Orange County, California, and is recognized as a mentor and expert in the field. He runs real estate seminars and online courses for aspiring investors. Despite personal challenges, including his battle with cancer and a public divorce, he continues to grow professionally.

I first sent Tarek "One Jordan" after my friend Cris Cawley managed to get his shoe size for me. Once Tarek received the shoe, he reached out, and we arranged a date to record a podcast. Unfortunately, we had to cancel our original date due to a family illness he was dealing with. If you follow Tarek on social media, you'll know he has an insanely busy schedule. I continued to follow up with his assistant, Brittany, because I was eager to include his story in this book. After a few months, his publicist expressed concerns about a potential conflict with the release dates of our books (he was releasing a book as well) and Tarek's busy schedule.

Consequently, Tarek's publicist informed me that, unfortunately, Tarek would be unable to participate in the podcast at that time, possibly later, which meant he wouldn't be in the book. Initially, I was disappointed, but then I understood that this was part of the process. I completely respected their decision to wait to do the podcast.

At this point, I had to pivot. I had already sent the "One Jordan," but what next? Should I ask for it back? Or should we just wait until we could record in the future and then send the second Jordan? I decided to go ahead and send the other shoe with a note saying, *"Tarek, please enjoy the Jordans. I'm sure we'll connect at a later date."* I then chose to move on and complete the book without his chapter.

As luck would have it, a couple of weeks later, I received an email that a time slot had opened up on Tarek's calendar, and he would love to be on my podcast if it wasn't too late. I was so excited to be able to include him in this book. My follow-up and follow-through worked. I didn't let the fear of rejection get in the way and continued communicating with the publicist.

During our conversation, we unpacked how it all started for him in real estate and his struggles. Tarek overcame every challenge imaginable. Going broke, living in his mother's garage, surviving cancer, not once but twice, economic downturns, people not believing in him, and his battles with alcohol.

We started our conversation discussing the greatest lesson he had ever learned. Tarek said, *"Everything we are told and taught is wrong. We have such amazing talents and abilities, but we are told early to stay in our lane and behave. Listening to that limits our self-belief and mindset because we are told not to do things."* He shared a powerful real-life example: the things that got him into the most trouble while growing up are what made him successful today. These include talking too much, asking adults too many questions, and constantly pushing boundaries. He said, "The skill set of not being afraid to talk or ask questions as a child became an incredible advantage as an adult."

Tarek believes he is a lucky guy. He has been through much personal pain and struggles in his life. Combined with his business and professional success, he is able to teach his children life lessons that give them a massive head start. Again, this is another example of Tarek's resolve and self-awareness playing a vital role in his unmatched success in real estate.

The next question I asked Tarek was, "What are you learning now?"

His response was simple. "I'm learning more about myself. Starting as a young entrepreneur, money was, of course, the driving force." His only concern was how he could make more money.

Regarding entrepreneurship, Tarek explained, "Making money is different from being educated. When it comes to traditional education, if you want to be a doctor or lawyer, you need the appropriate education, or they won't let you in. The U.S. education system does not teach us how to make money. Our country is essentially nothing more than a big company doing business with other countries worldwide. If everyone was taught the path of entrepreneurship, who would do all the other jobs to run the country? If people want to be financially free, they must invest in themselves."

At this point in his life, with so much financial and professional success, Tarek's priorities had changed. He is more excited about helping others and sharing his love of real estate to help others improve their lives, which has become his priority. Tarek is extremely generous and shares a great deal of wisdom and foresight pertaining to real estate for free on social media. This is an example of free education that ultimately results in making money.

"How has failure shaped your life?"

"If it weren't for failure," said Tarek, *"we would have zero success."*

Starting in real estate in his early 20s, Tarek experienced essentially six months with no business. That's when he hired a coach. (Side note: If the rest of this story doesn't convince you that you need a coach, I wish you luck. You'll need it.) His coach put him on a rigorous schedule: working twelve hours a day for six days a week, plus three hours on Sunday. You're probably wondering what a realtor would do for that many hours a day. The answer is calling expired listings, which are listings other realtors had but didn't sell. Essentially, this meant cold-calling clients. Tarek had to have fifty conversations a day, not just fifty phone calls, but actual conversations, before he could call it quits. After ninety days, Tarek had made $150,000 in commissions. At twenty-one years old, he was living in a million-dollar house, a significant upgrade from his mother's garage.

The first lesson he learned was that hard work pays off. However, just three short years later, he had to sell it all. Tarek found himself living in a run-down apartment, driving his dad's truck—which he borrowed and had no air conditioning and crank windows—a far cry from his previous Escalade, Mercedes, and lifestyle. This experience marked the first time Tarek hit rock bottom.

Finally, Tarek and I began breaking down how he went from rock bottom to *Flip or Flop*. This is one of the most amazing stories I've ever heard. Tarek and his ex-wife decided to attend a real estate conference in Las Vegas. Two seats opened up in the VIP section next to a friend, so his friend snuck them into the seats. If you've listened to me speak about any of the conferences I've attended, you'll know I always try to sit in the VIP section to meet the new "who's" in my life to help move the needle. This is exactly what Tarek was doing.

Get your highlighter out because you'll want to highlight this next part. While on a break in the VIP section, Tarek connected with an individual he had seen speaking the day before, who had told a story about making $800,000 from a television show. Tarek did what he does best, and if you remember the things that got him in trouble in his youth, he asked the gentleman on stage way too many questions. He realized that a television show would be the best marketing you could have in real estate. We all know that people do business with people they know, like, and trust. If you see me on television, there's an excellent chance you will know, like, and trust me.

If you're anything like me, when I return from a conference or seminar, I am on fire with all the new ideas and tactics I've learned. You know, the pages of notes and everything you've highlighted and journaled about the event. Unfortunately, it usually ends up being another stack of papers on our desk that impedes doing what we need to do. So hold on to your seats because what Tarek did next is a textbook example of how it's supposed to happen. Oh, by the way, did you know that when Tarek pitched the idea for *Flip or Flop,* he had never flipped a home? True story.

Sitting on the couch the night he returned from the conference, Tarek told his ex-wife he wanted to do a television show. She asked the million-dollar question, "About what?"

Tarek responded, "Flipping houses."

She laughed and went to bed, while Tarek stayed up all night, sending his idea to several Hollywood production companies. The following day, someone responded. They asked him to shoot a quick home video of his idea, which then turned into a two-day shoot for a sizzle reel, which they submitted to any network they could. Think about this for a moment: he received a response within twenty-four hours. Tarek must have felt a surge of excitement, thinking his idea was about to take off. And then, nothing. For ten months, there was silence.

"I had given up on the dream," said Tarek.

Then, in 2011, HGTV reached out and wanted to film a pilot. Once the pilot was completed, they told him he had a very slim chance of it becoming a successful television show. Weeks later, he got a contract from HGTV to flip thirteen houses in ten months on national TV. What a massive win; a literal dream come true. However, two rather large obstacles stood in his way: he didn't know *how* to flip houses, and he had no money to invest. Tarek took the contract to his attorney, who he had on retainer—and who, by the way, was on a payment plan. His question was, "What's the worst thing that can happen if I can't fulfill this contract?"

His attorney replied, "Well, they can sue you."

Tarek told me he thought about it, looked around his apartment and thought, *They can have it,* and that's how *Flip or Flop* was born.

What followed for Tarek was a massive amount of consistent action. We only see his accomplishments on TV. Let's summarize what it took for Tarek to succeed with this show. Initially, he worked eighteen to twenty hours a day. Per his contract, the only homes he could buy had to be vacant. Tarek would get a list of homes to be auctioned off and drive all over Southern California to check if they were occupied. What time are most people home?—between 10:00 p.m. and 4:00 a.m. That's when Tarek searched for vacant homes. These are the unseen hours, what he does in the dark when we're not watching. This is the difference between merely having a dream and actively working for it. Like Tarek said, "Through massive action, once in a while, you're gonna get lucky."

Note: This chapter is my summary of one of my favorite podcasts. If you enjoyed this chapter, check out the actual *One Hand at a Time* podcast, episode 29.

Mental Activity for Personal Growth

1. Tarek overcame numerous personal and professional challenges, including health and financial struggles. How does his journey inspire resilience, and what can you learn from his approach to overcoming obstacles?

_____

_____

_____

2. Tarek attributes much of his success to his childhood traits of asking questions and pushing boundaries. How can embracing these qualities be beneficial in adult life and professional endeavors?

_____

_____

_____

3. Tarek views failure as an essential component of success. How does his perspective challenge the fear of failure, and what lessons can be learned from his hard work and perseverance?

_____

_____

_____

4. As Tarek's career evolved, his priorities shifted from making money to helping others. How do personal values and priorities typically evolve with success, and how has this played out in your life or career?

_____

_____

_____

5. Reflecting on the "unseen hours" Tarek put in that often go unnoticed. How does this concept apply to your understanding of success, and how might it change your approach to your goals?

_____

_____

_____

6. Tarek is passionate about sharing his real estate knowledge for free on social media. Discuss the importance of sharing knowledge and expertise in your field. How can this approach benefit both the individual and the wider community?

_____

_____

_____

Conclusion

I hope you are excited about using the "One Jordan" method or a similar approach. I have shared these stories to demonstrate my successes and failures, all resulting from the sending of a single shoe. What's your plan? Do you have your list yet? Will you send "One Jordan" or something else? Will you adapt the strategy of R&D (rip-off and duplicate) and make it your own? This strategy can be applied to other gifts as well.

In my early years of originating loans, I would send a book titled *Time Traps* by Todd Duncan, along with a handwritten note and a $20 bill. The note read, "*Please accept the $20 for the time you spend reading this letter. I will call you on this date and time to connect and discuss the strategies I learned from Time Traps.*" I used this strategy to land the largest luxury realtor in my market.

Side note: I had been originating loans for only three months. Another strategy Rene Rodriguez shared was to buy a burner phone, charge it, turn it on, and send it in a FedEx package. When you receive proof of delivery, call the phone.

Before we wrap up, let's talk about whom you should put on the list. I didn't think my first list was big enough to worry about rejection. *Who am I to send this person a shoe?*—Don't sell yourself short. This week (while I write this), "One Jordan" was sent to Ed Mylett and John Maxwell, absolute titans in the peak performance and leadership worlds. Make sure you have a plan for when it *works* and what you will do next. If I can make connections with my "One Jordan" list, imagine what you can do. You now have the blueprint and the proof that it works. The next move is yours.

Mental Activity for Personal Growth

1. Decide on what you will send to capture the attention. Brainstorm as many items as possible. Make it your own and take action today.

_____

_____

_____

_____

_____

2. How will you find the contact information? Who do you know who may know someone on your list?

_____

_____

_____

Final Thoughts

I want to hear from you. Please share with me how you will connect to the individuals on your list. Use the #onejordanbook and tag our IG @onejordanbook. We've created the "One Jordan" Group pages on IG and Facebook as a community to share your journey.

Follow me @onehandatatime and @onejordanbook on IG. Join our Facebook group "One Jordan" Book and our websites WWW.Chriswelton.live and www.onejordanbook.com, and check out my podcast, *One Hand at a Time*.

THANK YOU FOR READING MY BOOK!

Thank you for reading my book! Here are a few free bonus gifts.

Scan the QR Code Here:

I appreciate your interest in my book and value your feedback as it helps me improve future versions of this book. I would appreciate it if you could leave your invaluable review on Amazon.com with your feedback. Thank you!

www.ingramcontent.com/pod-product-compliance
Lightning Source LLC
Chambersburg PA
CBHW052120090426
42741CB00009B/1884